INVENTORS AT WORK!

The Woman Who Invented Windshield Wipers

Mary Anderson and Her Wonderful Invention

Sara L. Latta

Enslow Elementary
an imprint of
Enslow Publishers, Inc.
40 Industrial Road
Box 398
Berkeley Heights, NJ 07922
USA
http://www.enslow.com

Enslow Elementary, an imprint of Enslow Publishers, Inc.

Enslow Elementary® is a registered trademark of Enslow Publishers, Inc.

Library of Congress Cataloging-in-Publication Data

Latta, Sara L.
 The woman who invented windshield wipers : Mary Anderson and her wonderful invention / by Sara Latta.
 pages cm. — (Inventors at work!)
  Summary: "Read about Mary Anderson's early life, and find out why she invented windshield wipers"—
  Provided by publisher.
Includes bibliographical references and index.
  ISBN 978-0-7660-4203-2
 1. Anderson, Mary, 1866-1953—Juvenile literature. 2. Women inventors—United States—Juvenile literature.
  3. Inventors—United States—Juvenile literature. 4. Windshield wipers—Juvenile literature. I. Anderson,
  Mary, 1866-1953 II. Title.
 T40.A53L38 2014
 629.2'76—dc23
 [B]
                                        2012041916

Future editions:
Paperback ISBN: 978-1-4644-0349-1
EPUB ISBN: 978-1-4645-1193-6
Single-User PDF ISBN: 978-1-4646-1193-3
Multi-User PDF ISBN: 978-0-7660-5825-5

Printed in the United States of America

10 9 8 7 6 5 4 3 2

To Our Readers: We have done our best to make sure all Internet addresses in this book were active and appropriate when we went to press. However, the author and the publisher have no control over and assume no liability for the material available on those Internet sites or on other Web sites they may link to. Any comments or suggestions can be sent by e-mail to comments@enslow.com or to the address on the back cover.

♻ Enslow Publishers, Inc., is committed to printing our books on recycled paper. The paper in every book contains 10% to 30% post-consumer waste (PCW). The cover board on the outside of each book contains 100% PCW. Our goal is to do our part to help young people and the environment too!

Photo Credits: Birmingham Public Library Archives, p. 8; © Caro/Alamy, p. 4; Jupiterimages/Thinkstock, pp. 12, 29; Courtesy Birmingham Public Library, p. 22; Courtesy of New York Transit Museum, p. 18; Fresno City & County Historical Society Archives, p. 14; Hemera/Thinkstock, p. 38 (limo); imagebroker.net/SuperStock, p. 38 (futuristic trucks); © iStockphoto.com/Loretta Hostettler, p. 33; iStockphoto/Thinkstock, p. 38 (helicopter, rear windshield,train); Library of Congress, Prints and Photographs, pp. 20, 27; Missouri History Museum, St. Louis, p. 6; © Mouse in the House/Alamy, p. 39 (glasses); NASA/JPL-Caltech, p. 36 (bottom); National Automotive History Collection, Detroit Public Library, p. 10; Nicole deMilla, p. 31; Shi Yali/Shutterstock.com, p. 39 (high-speed train); Shutterstock.com, pp. 15, 16, 35, 39 (plane, ferry boat, bus, trucks), 40, 41, 42, 43; United States Patent Office, p. 25; Univ Carlos III of Madrid, p. 36 (top).

Cover Photo: Mary Anderson: Courtesy Birmingham Public Library; Illustration of car: Shutterstock.com

CONTENTS

Can you imagine a car without windshield wipers? They are so important to help drivers see the road in rain and snow.

A Southern Life

When it rains or snows, drivers turn on their windshield wipers. Swish-swash, left to right, the wipers dance, back and forth. They wipe away rain, snow, and sleet so that cab drivers, bus drivers—all kinds of drivers—can see clearly.

Imagine a car without windshield wipers! As a matter of fact, the earliest automobiles had no windshields at all. Driving goggles came in very handy in those days.

The first car windshield, introduced in 1904, could be folded down if it became so dirty that drivers could not see through it. The only way to clean the glass was to wipe it by hand.

Drivers of early cars wore goggles to protect their eyes. This car was made in 1906.

When Mary Anderson saw a streetcar driver doing just that, she thought there had to be a better way. And so, the Southern belle invented the windshield wiper.

Born on a Plantation

Mary Anderson was born in Greene County, Alabama. She was the daughter of plantation owners. There is little known about her childhood. We do know that she was born on February 19, 1866. This year was a time of great change for the country. The Civil War had ended less than a year earlier.

Mary's parents, John and Rebecca Anderson, owned their Burton Hill Plantation. Mary's father died when she was just four years old. Now it was up to her mother to manage the plantation and to care for Mary and her sister Fannie. When Mary Anderson was twenty-three years old, the family moved to Birmingham, Alabama. This was about ninety miles away.

Mary Anderson and her family built and lived in this Fairmont Apartment building in Birmingham, Alabama.

A New Life in Birmingham

Rebecca Anderson and her daughters built the Fairmont Apartment building. They were in a very nice suburb of Birmingham. Now they had a place to live. They also got money from the people who rented the apartments.

The apartment building gave Mary the freedom that not many women had at that time. Most women were expected to marry or take low-paying jobs to make money. And it would be thirty years until women were even given the right to vote! Mary must have had many chances to meet young men in Birmingham's busy social scene. But she had other ideas.

Fold-down windshields allowed drivers to see when the windshield got too dirty. But Mary Anderson had a better idea!

The Land of Dreams

Mary Anderson must have had a great sense of adventure. In 1893, when she was twenty-seven, she moved to Fresno, California. Many young women would have taken a typical woman's job at the time, such as teaching. Not Anderson. She ran a cattle ranch and vineyard!

We don't know much about what drew Anderson to California, or what happened during those years. But many people thought of California as the land of dreams.

The Alabama Colony

Shortly after the Civil War, there was a group of Alabama planters looking for a fresh start. They began a farming

"Boys, I believe I have found a gold mine!" When news of gold in California got out in 1848, thousands of people poured into the state. They hoped that, with hard work and a little luck, they would get rich quick. Most did not. But decades later, California was still seen as a place where people could find fame and fortune.

colony near Fresno. The Alabama colony had failed by the time Anderson arrived in Fresno. These Southern plantation owners had been used to growing cotton. Now they had to learn to raise other crops. The climate was different. They had to pay workers.

Perhaps Anderson knew some of the founders of the Alabama colony. We do know that land developers in the area urged the "independent woman" to invest in and manage a small farm, growing raisins or orchard fruits. To take care of any "rough work in the fields," the article said, "all such labor may be done by men hired in season."

A Surprise Treasure

Anderson stayed in Fresno just five years. She moved back to Birmingham to help care for her sick aunt. The aunt moved into their apartment, bringing with her seventeen large trunks. The aunt insisted on keeping all the trunks in her room. Once a week, she asked Mary to open the trunks and take out the trays "so that auntie

Many people tried to make a new life by farming in California.

may look by herself." There was just one rule: Anderson had to do it with her eyes closed.

When the aunt died a few years later, Anderson and her family looked inside the mysterious trunks. They were filled with gold, jewels, and other treasures. Anderson, her mother, and sister shared the aunt's fortune.

real fact!

When Mary Anderson and her family moved to Birmingham in 1889, most people traveled by horse-drawn carriages. Just five years earlier, steam-powered streetcars began to run throughout the city. This made it easier for people who lived in the Birmingham suburbs to get to work in the downtown area.

A Snowy Day in New York City

In the winter of 1902 or 1903, Mary Anderson used some of her money to visit New York City. One cold and snowy day, Anderson was riding an electric streetcar. There was so much to see!

Anderson must have marveled at the sights of the big city. But there was one sight that bothered her. Slushy snow piled up on the windshields of the streetcars. This made it impossible for the streetcar drivers to see outside. She noticed that the drivers often had to stop, get out, and clean the windows by hand. The drivers had only two choices. They could keep the windshield down, letting the cold snow and

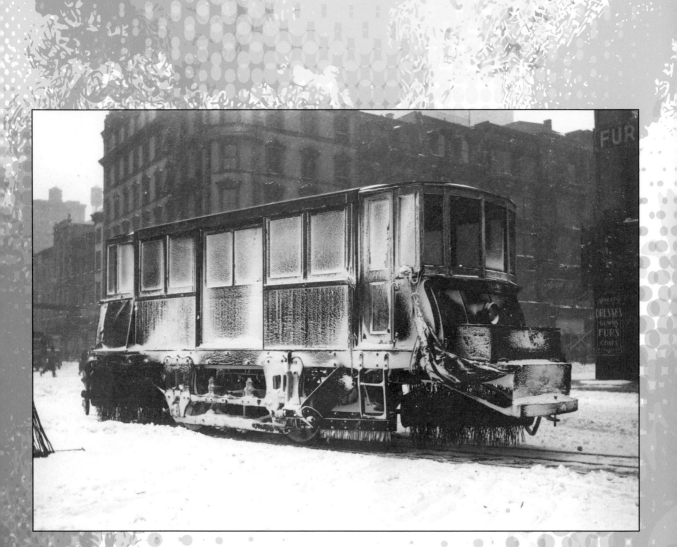

When Anderson was riding the streetcars in New York City, she was bothered by the snow and sleet piling up on the windshields. She decided to invent a way to clean them.

sleet in. Or, they could lean out of the side window to clear the glass. Either way, the driver (and sometimes the passengers) got cold and wet.

Anderson felt sorry for the streetcar drivers. As a Southerner, she was not used to the cold. If she was cold, imagine how uncomfortable the drivers must be!

Anderson asked why someone didn't make a tool to clear the glass—one that didn't require the driver to leave the car. Time and time again, people told her it couldn't be done.

Drivers tried all sorts of things to keep their windshields clear in bad weather. One common solution was to rub a cut onion, a slice of carrot, or a plug of tobacco over the windshield. The idea was that these things would leave an oily film on the glass. This was supposed to prevent water from collecting. Not surprisingly, this method did not work very well. Mostly, it left a stinky mess.

A split windshield could be opened in the middle.
But then the driver would get wet with rain or snow.

The best idea the experts came up with was a split windshield that could be opened in the middle. The driver could see—but only if he didn't mind being drenched with rain or snow.

Mary Anderson thought there had to be a better way to keep the windshield clear.

A Window Cleaning Device Takes Shape

Back in Birmingham, Anderson could not get those cold, wet streetcar drivers out of her head. She took out her sketchbook and began to draw a picture of the gadget she had in mind.

Her "window cleaning device," as she called it, had a spring-loaded wooden arm with a rubber blade that could sweep across the windshield. The arm was attached to a lever near the steering wheel of the car. The driver could use the lever to move the arm back and forth across the windshield. A weight attached to the arm held it firmly against the windshield. Anderson

This photograph of Mary Anderson was taken around the time that she came up with the idea for her windshield cleaning device.

even designed the device so that it could be removed during fair weather.

Mary Anderson took her drawing to a company in Birmingham and asked them to make a model for her.

Anderson's Patent

On November 10, 1903, Anderson received Patent number 743,801 for her "Window Cleaning Device." In 1905, she tried to sell her design to a company in Canada. The company was known for buying patents and making new devices. If they bought her patent and the wipers caught on with drivers, she could make a lot of money. Instead, she received a letter from the firm, saying, " . . . we do not consider it to be of such commercial value as would warrant our undertaking its sale." In other words, Madam, we don't believe anybody will want to buy your gadget.

Anderson must have felt bad that she could not sell her invention. Couldn't people see how it would make driving in bad weather easier and safer?

This is the drawing of the "Window Cleaning Device" that Anderson sent to the U.S. Patent Office. In her patent application, she gave detailed descriptions of how each part of the device worked. The illustration helped Anderson explain her idea.

Although her drawing was very specific, she said that the design could be changed to suit the builder's needs "without departing from the spirit and scope of my invention." Anderson did not want anybody to make small changes to her patent and then claim that they had invented something different!

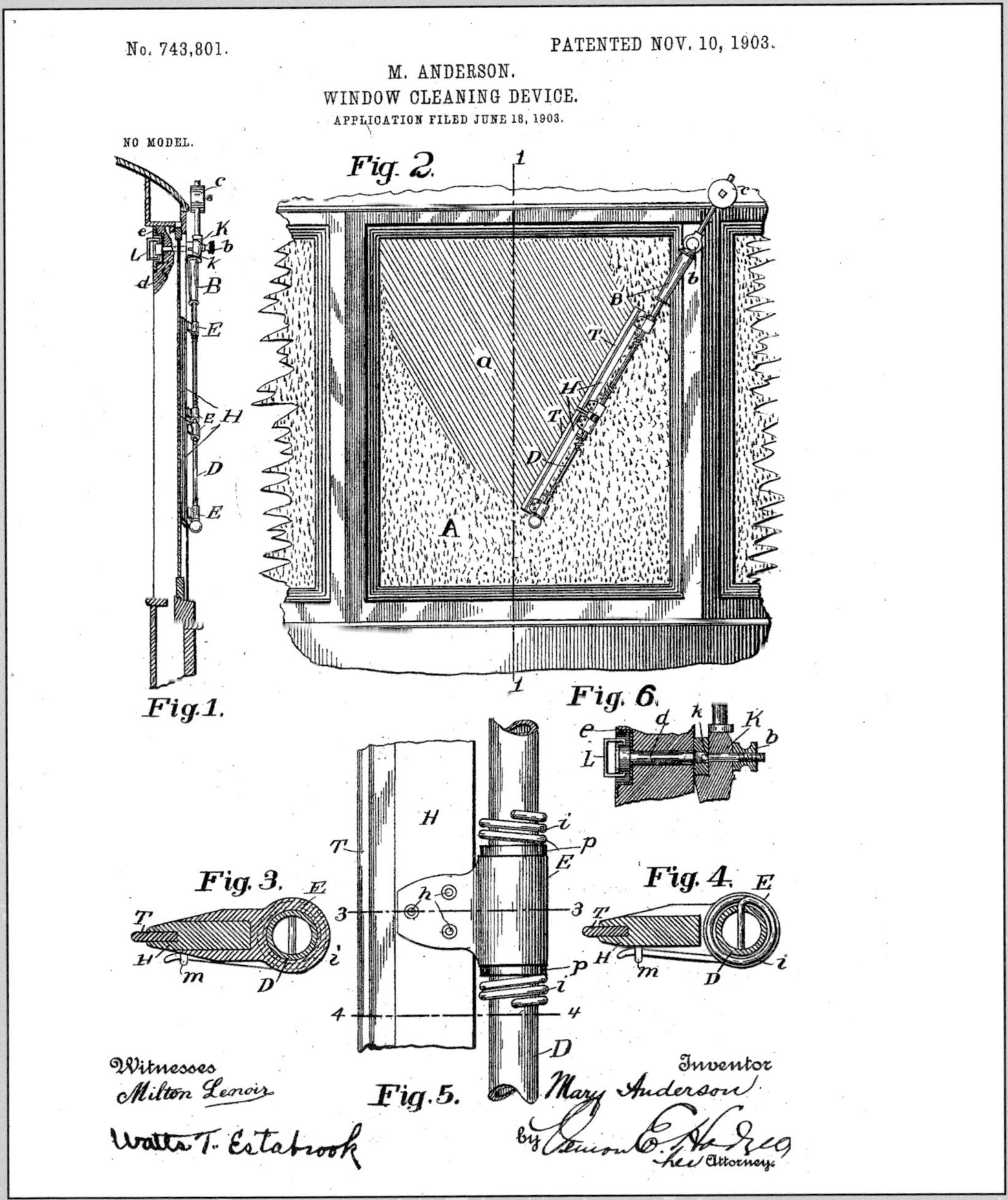

No. 743,801.

PATENTED NOV. 10, 1903.

M. ANDERSON.
WINDOW CLEANING DEVICE.
APPLICATION FILED JUNE 18, 1903.

NO MODEL.

Fig. 2.

Fig. 1.

Fig. 6.

Fig. 3.

Fig. 4.

Fig. 5.

Witnesses
Milton Lenoir
Walter T. Estabrook

Inventor
Mary Anderson
by Cemon E. Hodge
her Attorney.

Mary Anderson's patent included a picture of her invention.

"Oh, So Impractical!"

Most of Anderson's friends seemed to agree with the Canadian company. Some even teased her. They called her "oh, so impractical." After all, there were not many cars on the roads in 1905. Some people made fun of car owners. Others hated cars because they were loud. They sometimes backfired and scared the horses. One doctor believed that traveling "15 to 20 miles an hour in a motor car" could cause serious health problems for women.

Other people thought that the back-and-forth movement of the wipers would be dangerous. They believed it would take the driver's attention away from the road and could lead to accidents.

At any rate, the earliest cars had no windshield anyway. They did not go fast enough to need one.

Perhaps Anderson believed the doubters. Maybe she was just too busy helping manage her apartment building. Whatever the reason, she did not try to sell her idea to any other company. She let the patent expire.

Because there were not many cars on the roads in 1905, some people called Mary Anderson's invention impractical. This scene is in Washington, D.C.

The Model T Revolution

In 1908, Henry Ford started making the Model T. He changed the way Americans felt about cars. Before, people thought of cars as big toys for rich people. Ford wanted to make a car "so low in price that no man making a good salary will be unable to own one."

At first the Model T cost $850. As Ford got better at making the car, it got even cheaper. The Model T was not just cheap. It was well built. People could depend on it to run. It was a great success.

After that, Americans learned to love the car. In 1905, there were only 77,000 cars in the United States. By 1910, that number had risen to 500,000. Just

The Model T was a great success! Many people were now driving cars, and the need for windshield wipers grew.

five years later, there were 2.3 million cars in the country! There were a lot of cars on the road—and a greater need for good windshield wipers.

Wipers in Action

There were other attempts to make windshield wipers. One used two brushes that moved up and down the windshield. None of the ideas was very successful.

In 1916, a man named John R. Oishei had an accident. It changed his life. He was driving his car one rainy night in Buffalo, New York, when he hit a man riding a bicycle. The man was not badly hurt, but Oishei was upset. He vowed to find a better way to keep the windshield clear. He founded a company, the Tri-Continental Corporation (later called Trico), to make windshield wipers.

Like Anderson's invention, his wipers also had to be worked by hand. But, unlike Anderson, he was able to sell his product. He went on to make a fortune making windshield wipers. In fact, Trico still makes windshield wipers.

The Trico windshield wipers are still made today.

Making a Better Wiper

All of the hand-operated wipers shared one big problem. The driver had to crank the wipers with one hand, and steer and shift the gears with the other. Think about how unsafe this might be in the pouring rain!

A Canadian stage actress named Charlotte Bridgwood invented the first automatic windshield wiper in 1917. Her Storm Windshield Cleaner used rollers rather than blades. It was powered by an electric motor. Bridgwood was a successful businesswoman, but she was no more successful than Anderson at selling her invention.

Bridgwood's daughter Florence Lawrence, a silent movie star, may have helped her mother design the wiper. She loved to drive. She also invented the first turning and braking signals for cars.

In the board game Trivial Pursuit, "Mary Anderson" is the correct answer to the question "What woman invented the windshield wiper in 1903?"

Windshield Wipers Everywhere

By the 1940s and 1950s, most cars had windshield wipers. Chrysler brought out electric wipers in 1940. They moved at the same speed no matter how hard it was raining. A few years later, wipers had two settings: one for steady rain and one for very heavy rain. In 1967, a man named Robert Kearns invented a wiper that would go on and off at different speeds—like a "blinking eye," he said.

Today, some cars have wipers on the rear window and on the headlights. Some models even have wipers that can sense rain and turn themselves on at the right speed.

Windshield wipers will soon even make it to outer space. Scientists have developed a windshield wiper to move dust from the sensors of spacecraft bound for Mars.

By the 1950s, windshield wipers were an important part of all cars.

A Long and Happy Life

The windshield wiper was Mary Anderson's one brush with fame. She continued to manage her apartment building until she died in 1953 at her summer home in Tennessee. She was eighty-seven years old. Anderson

NASA scientists have built windshield wipers (top) to wipe dust from spacecraft (bottom) that are sent to explore Mars.

never made a penny from her invention, but she led a full and happy life.

Still, there must have been times when she wished she had worked a little harder to sell her invention. After all, by the time she died, every driver was familiar with the swish-swish sound of the windshield wiper on a rainy day.

Windshield Wipers Are Now Found in Many Places!

rear wiper, limo

helicopter

rear wiper, car

futuristic trucks, Germany

train

glasses

high-speed trains

ferry boat

airplane

SCHOOL BUS

bus

trucks

So you want to be an inventor? You can do it! First, you need a terrific idea.

Got a Problem? No Problem!

Many inventions begin when someone thinks of a great solution to a problem. One cold day in 1994, ten-year-old K. K. Gregory was building a snow fort. Soon, she had snow between her mittens and her coat sleeve. Her wrists were cold and wet. She found some scraps of fabric around the house, and used them to make a tube that would fit around her wrist. She cut a thumb hole in the tube to make a kind of fingerless glove, and called it a "Wristie." Wearing mittens over her new invention, her wrists stayed nice and warm when she played outside. Today, the Wristie business is booming.

Now it's your turn. Maybe, like K. K. Gregory, you have an idea for something new that would make your life better or easier. Perhaps you can think of a way to improve an everyday item. Twelve-year-old Becky Schroeder became one of the youngest people ever to receive a U.S. patent after she invented a glow-in-the-dark clipboard that allowed people to write in the dark. Do you like to play sports or board games? James Naismith, inspired by a game he used to play as a boy, invented a new game he called basketball.

Let your imagination run wild. You never know where it will take you.

Research It!

Okay, you have a terrific idea for an invention. Now what do you do?

First, you'll want to make sure that nobody else has

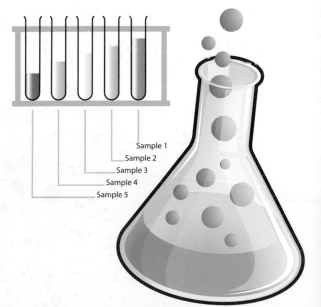

Sample 1
Sample 2
Sample 3
Sample 4
Sample 5

thought of your idea. You wouldn't want to spend hours developing your new invention only to find that someone else beat you to it. Check out Google Patents (see Learn More for the Web site address), which can help you find out whether your idea is original.

Bring It to Life!

If no one else has thought of your idea, congratulations! Write it down in a notebook. Date and initial every entry you make. If you file a patent for your invention later, this will help you prove that you were the first to think of it. The most important thing about this logbook is that pages cannot be added or subtracted. You can buy a bound notebook at any office supply store.

Draw several different pictures of your invention in your logbook. Try sketching views from above, below, and to the side. Show how big each part of your invention should be.

Build a model. Don't be discouraged if it doesn't work at first. You may have to experiment with different designs and materials. That's part of the fun! Take pictures of everything, and tape them into your logbook. Try your invention out on your friends and family. If they have any suggestions to make it better, build another model. Perfect your invention, and give it a clever name.

Patent It!

Do you want to sell your invention? You'll want to apply for a patent. Holding a patent to your invention means that no one else can make, use, or sell your invention in the United States without your permission. It 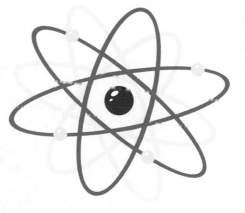 prevents others from making money off your idea. You will definitely need an adult to help you apply for a patent. It can be a complicated and expensive process. But if you think that people will want to buy your invention, it is well worth it. Good luck!

TIMELINE

1866 Mary Anderson is born in Greene County, Alabama, on February 19.

1893 Anderson moves to Fresno, California, to manage a vineyard and cattle ranch.

1898 Anderson moves back to Birmingham to help care for her aunt.

1902–1903 Anderson's winter visit to New York City inspires her to design the windshield wiper.

1903 Anderson is granted a patent (number 743801) for her "Window Cleaning Device" on November 10.

1904 The first car windshield is invented.

1908 Henry Ford begins making the Model T automobile.

1917 John R. Oishei founds the Tri–Continental Company to make windshield wipers.

Charlotte Bridgwood invents the first automatic windshield wiper.

1953 Mary Anderson dies at her summer home in Tennessee on June 27. She is eighty–seven years old.

WORDS TO KNOW

automatic—Describing a device or process that works by itself, with little or no help from a person.

Civil War—A war between the northern United States and the southern states that wanted to be separate from the North. The war lasted from 1861 to 1865. The South surrendered to the North.

commercial—Relating to a money-making business.

invention—An original device or process.

patent—An official paper that gives an inventor the only right to make, use, or sell an invention for a certain number of years.

sensor—A device that detects changes in the environment, such as temperature or light, and records or somehow responds to those changes.

LEARN MORE

Books

Braun, Sandra. *Incredible Women Inventors*. Toronto: Second Story Press, 2007.

Clements, Gillian. *The Picture History of Great Inventors*. London: Frances Lincoln Children's Books, 2005.

St. George, Judith. *So You Want to Be an Inventor?* New York: Puffin, 2005.

Sussman, Julie. *Dare to Repair Your Car: A Do-It-Herself Guide to Maintenance, Safety, Minor Fix-Its, and Talking Shop*. New York: William Morrow Paperbacks, 2005.

Williams, Marcia. *Hooray for Inventors!* Cambridge, Mass.: Candlewick Press, 2005.

LEARN MORE

Web Sites

If you want to learn more about becoming an inventor, check out these Web sites:

Google Patents. <http://google.com/patents>

Inventnow.org. <http://www.inventnow.org/>

The Inventive Kids Blog. <http://www.inventivekids .com/>

The U.S. Patent and Trademark Office for Kids. <http://www.uspto.gov/web/offices/ac/ahrpa/ opa/kids/index.html>

You can see a group of fifth graders doing the windshield wiper dance here: <http://www.youtube.com/watch?v=IujrtzJ4BF4>

INDEX